newprovidence
MEMORIAL LIBRARY

377 Elkwood Avenue
New Providence, NJ 07974

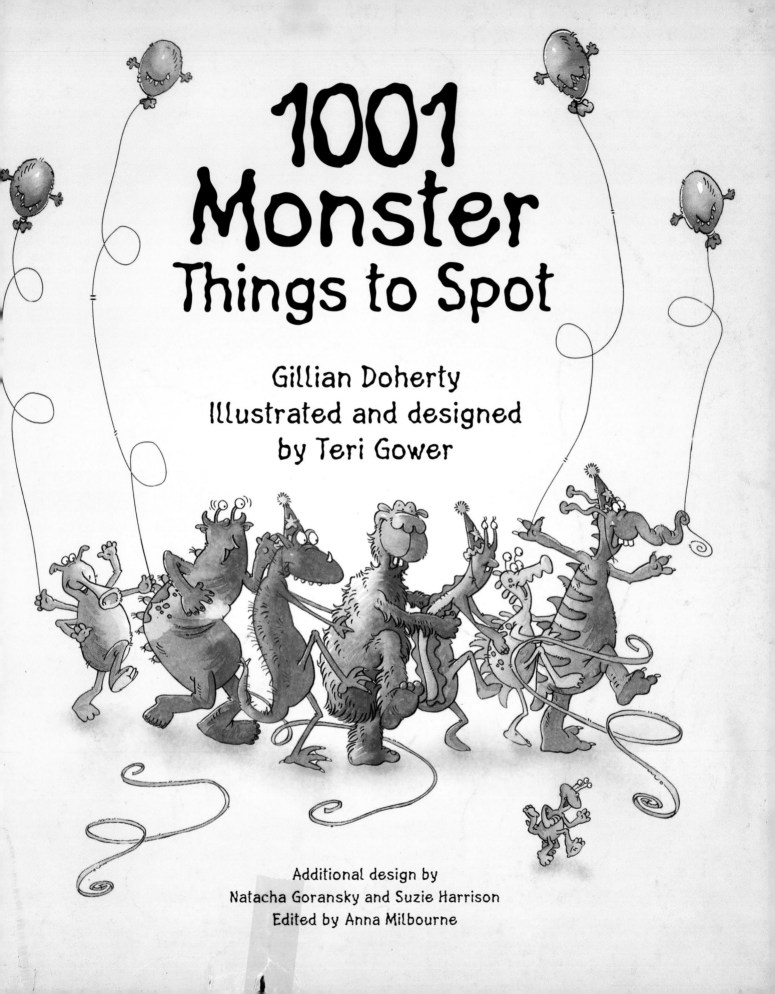

1001 Monster Things to Spot

Gillian Doherty
Illustrated and designed
by Teri Gower

Additional design by
Natacha Goransky and Suzie Harrison
Edited by Anna Milbourne

Contents

Things to Spot

Monsters come in all shapes and sizes. Most of them are very friendly, as you'll find out when you explore their monster world.

In each scene there are all kinds of monstrosities for you to find and count. There are 1001 things to spot altogether.

Monster Party

5 clodhoppers   6 trombugles   8 wowows   9 party hats   1 monstrous cake

8 monster poppers   10 monster balloons   9 boogaloos   6 striped presents   4 humdingers

26   27

Each little picture shows you what to look for in the big picture.

The number tells you how many of that thing you need to find.

Billy is crazy about monsters and when he grows up he wants to be a monsterologist. Can you find him tracking monsters in every scene?

Bedroom Monsters

5 astro monsters

7 slumber busters

6 pingles

8 bubble beasts

5 pocket trolls

10 sock eaters

3 toy rockets

6 doodle monsters

9 scufflebumps

Midnight Feast

7 nibblers

10 scoffits

9 monster muffins

8 gobblitos

4 bottles of monsterade

3 bellyphants

10 sticky buns

9 pot-bellied flimbos

6 chomps

5 towering sandwiches

Monster Nursery

10 roaring rattles   **5** toddling sproggles   **9** toy monsters   **7** fuzzy grizzles   **6** mollycoddles

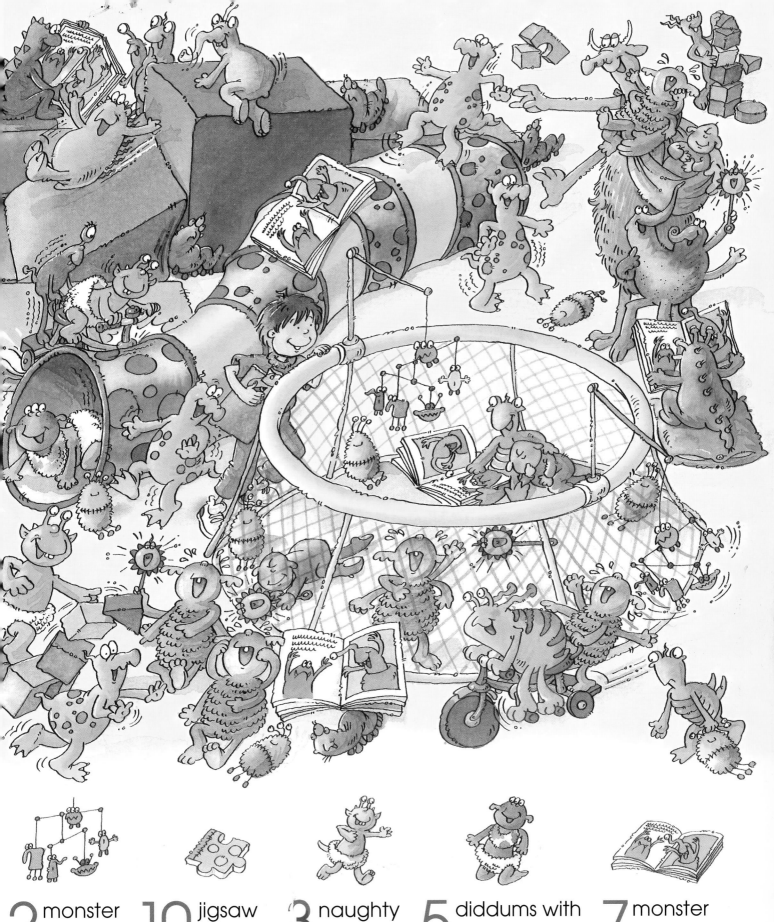

2 monster mobiles

10 jigsaw pieces

3 naughty ninkles

5 diddums with messy bibs

7 monster storybooks

Freaky Market

5 T-shirts with four arms **8** stink bombs **6** natterwags **7** people detectors **8** dawdlums

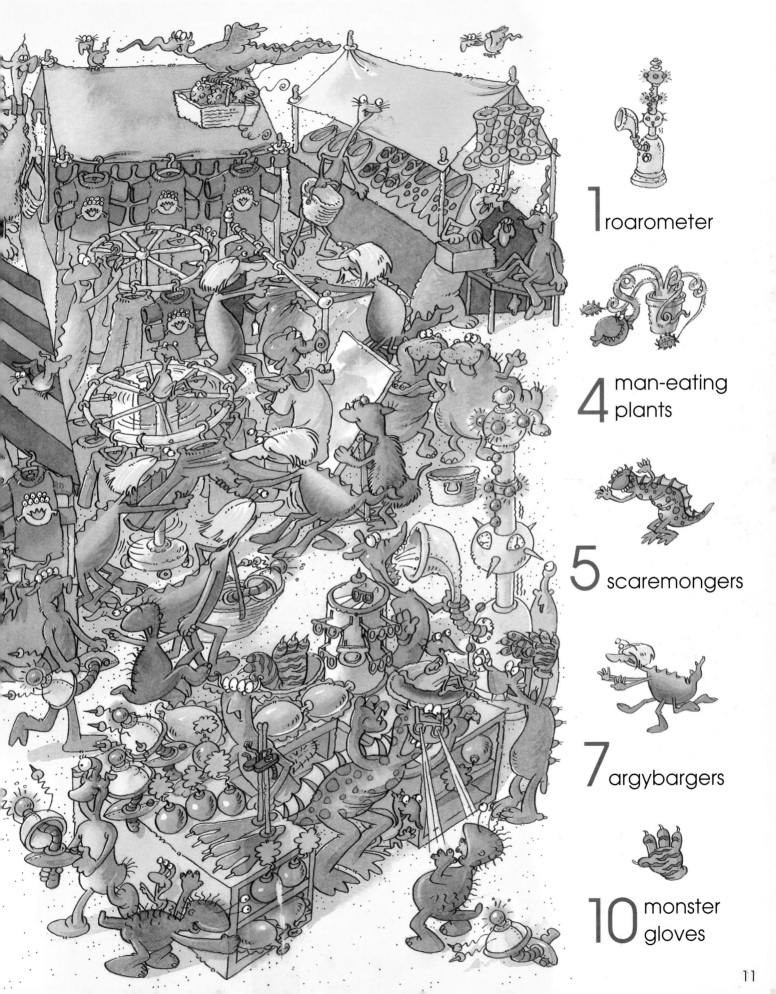

1 roarometer

4 man-eating plants

5 scaremongers

7 argybargers

10 monster gloves

Monster Park

5 monster kites

10 beastballers

1 monster cycle

2 three-headed dogs

7 boingy beasts

10 fuzzy frisbees   9 hopadoos   6 zoobers skating   3 quimbles on swings   5 hurlyburbles

Beastly School

4 misfangles **6** yellow munchboxes **8** swotty blots **9** school ties **7** one-eyed gumps

5 polkadot backpacks **7** scamps **9** paper planes **10** pen porters **6** quagvarks

Creepy Camp

7 snugglebugs

9 giant spiders

8 owligators

1 campfire

10 spooky lanterns

6 hairy howlers

3 growling guitars

10 monstrous shadows

9 buzzwings

8 shufflesnaps

17

Beach Beasts

6 merbeasts

10 rubber rings

6 giant sandcastles

9 craggles

8 beach balls

8 bobsurfers

10 furry fish

7 bloops

9 wingles

2 sea squibbles

Carnival Parade

1 huffalump

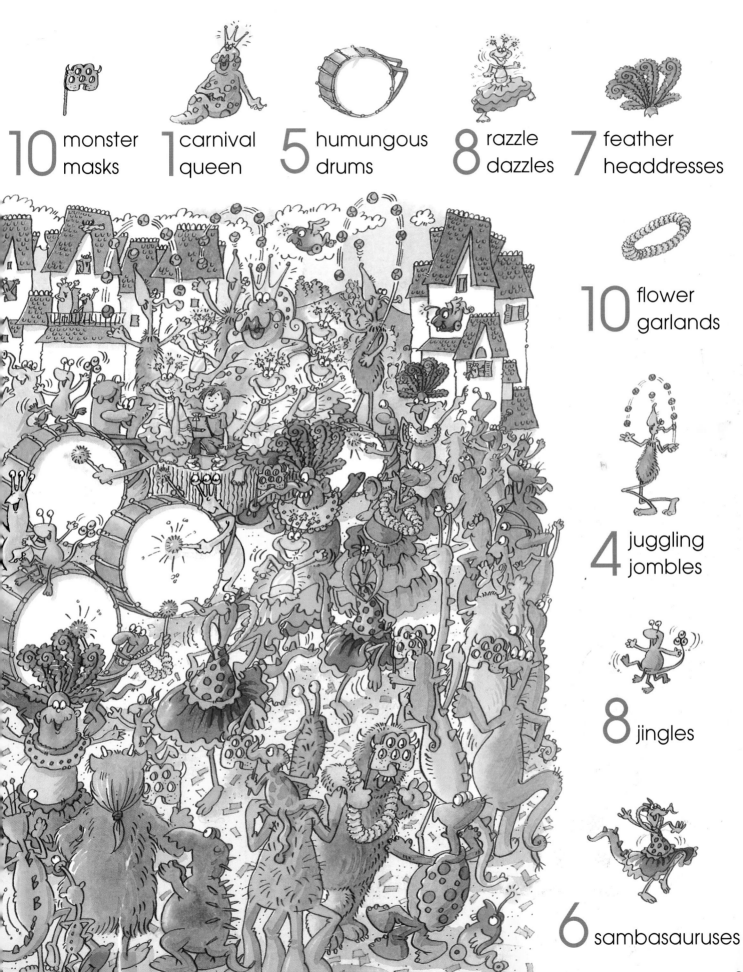

10 monster masks

1 carnival queen

5 humungous drums

8 razzle dazzles

7 feather headdresses

10 flower garlands

4 juggling jombles

8 jingles

6 sambasauruses

Monster Hospital

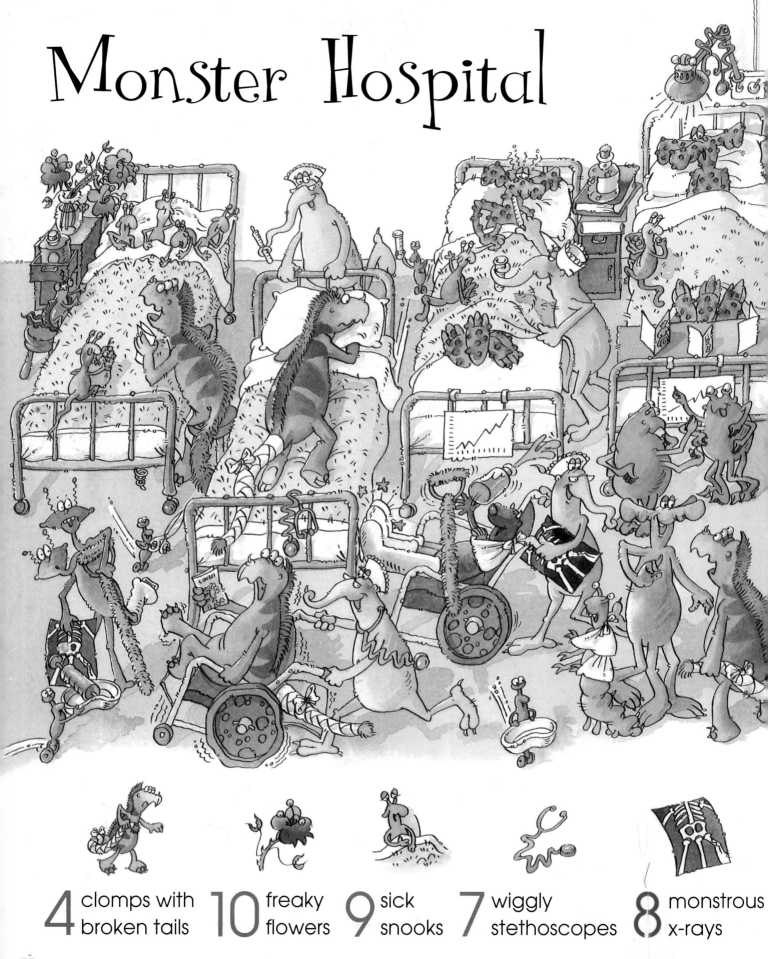

4 clomps with broken tails **10** freaky flowers **9** sick snooks **7** wiggly stethoscopes **8** monstrous x-rays

10 pootles 4 octodoctors 8 noddle nurses 5 wuffles with lumpitis 9 furry crutches

Beauty Salon

8 powder puffs

5 beasticians

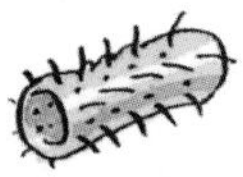

9 yellow rollers

10 bottles of claw varnish

7 ugly mugglies

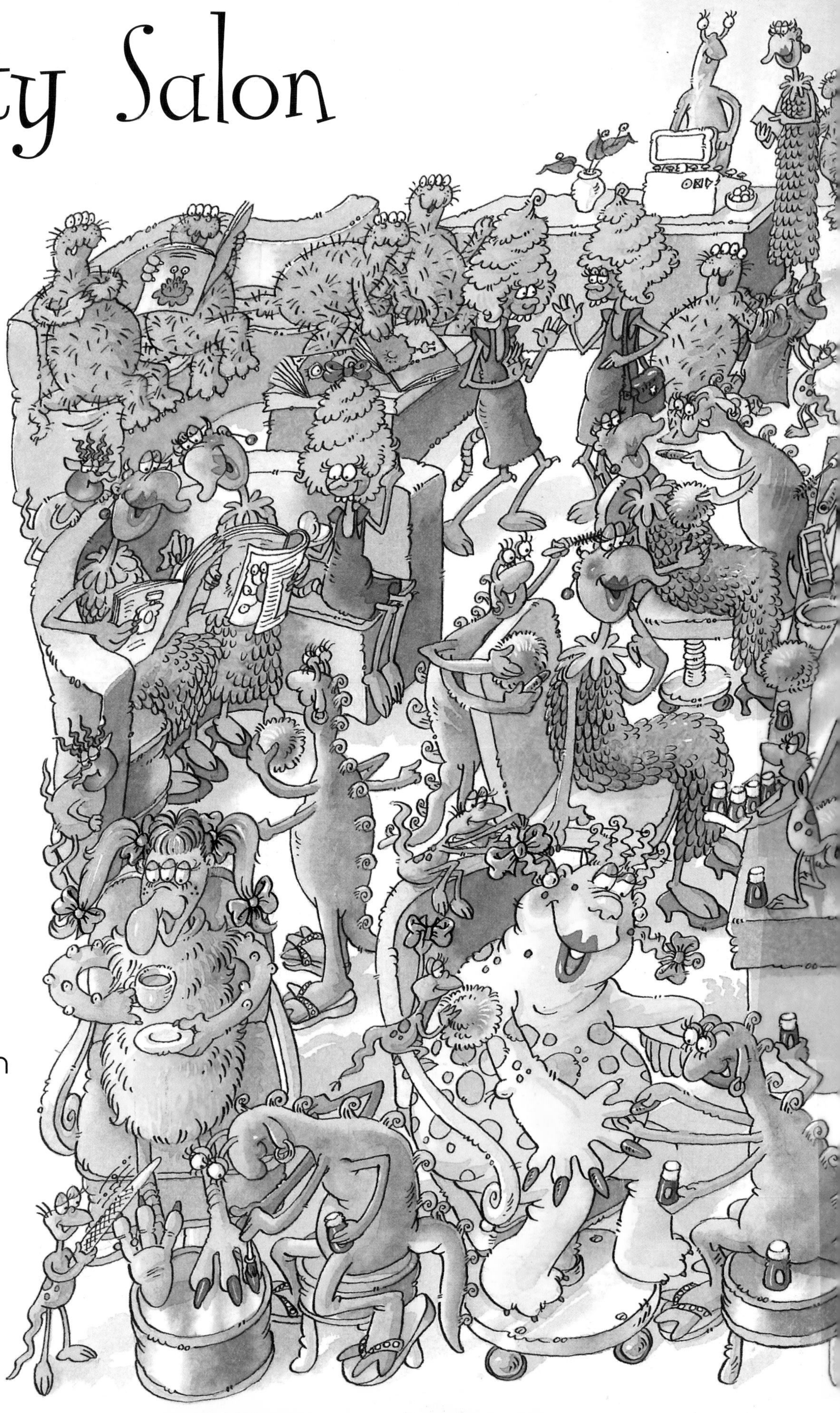

9 pink bows   4 monster furdryers   10 snippets   7 bigwigs   8 splendiferoos

Monster Party

5 clodhoppers   6 trombugles   8 wowows   9 party hats   1 monstrous cake

8 monster poppers   10 monster balloons   9 boogaloos   6 striped presents   4 humdingers

Snow Monsters

10 huge footprints

5 yetis

8 skidoobles

9 frostbiters

3 ice giants

10 snowballs

6 snow buggies

7 snozzlebird ski lifts

4 snow monsters

9 pairs of
earmuffs

Monster Gallery

Not all monsters are big and bold. Some are shy and tricky to spot. Billy's pictures of some of these bashful beasts are on show at the monster gallery. Can you find them throughout the book?

7 hushabillies

10 shadow huggers

6 phobies

8 skulks

9 heebie jeebies

6 dweebles

8 bashflubbers

10 jitterbugs

9 grimples

5 blushums

9 wheedles

7 peekaboos

8 quivers

Answers

Did you find all the shy monsters from the monster gallery? Here's where they are:

10 shadow huggers
Bedroom Monsters
(pages 4–5)

6 dweebles
Beastly School
(pages 14–15)

9 wheedles
Carnival Parade
(pages 20–21)

6 phobies
Freaky Market
(pages 10–11)

8 bashflubbers
Monster Park
(pages 12–13)

7 peekaboos
Monster Nursery
(pages 8–9)

8 skulks
Midnight Feast
(pages 6–7)

10 jitterbugs
Monster Party
(pages 26–27)

8 quivers
Beach Beasts
(pages 18–19)

7 hushabillies
Monster Hospital
(pages 22–23)

9 grimples
Snow Monsters
(pages 28–29)

9 heebie jeebies
Creepy Camp
(pages 16–17)

5 blushums
Beauty Salon
(pages 24–25)

First published in 2008 by Usborne Publishing Ltd.,
Usborne House, 83-85 Saffron Hill, London EC1N 8RT, England. www.usborne.co.uk
Copyright © 2008, Usborne Publishing Ltd. The name Usborne and the devices ⚇⚇ are Trade Marks of Usborne Publishing Ltd.
All rights reserved. No part of this publication may be reproduced, stored in a retrieval system, or transmitted in any form
or by any means, electronic, mechanical, photocopying, recording or otherwise, without the prior permission of the publisher.
First published in America in 2008. UE. Printed in China.

Pub- 17.99 8/09